MW01099076

Maryland

by Ed Pell

Consultant:
Cynthia Neverdon-Morton, Ph.D.
Professor of History and
Chairperson, Department of History,
Geography, and Global Studies
Coppin State College
Baltimore, Maryland

Capstone
press
Mankato, Minnesota

Capstone Press
151 Good Counsel Drive • P.O. Box 669 • Mankato, Minnesota 56002
http://www.capstone-press.com

Printed in the United States of America

Library of Congress Cataloging-in-Publication Data
Pell, Ed.
    Maryland/by Ed Pell.
    v.cm.—(Land of Liberty)
    Includes bibliographical references and index.
    Contents: About Maryland—Land, climate, wildlife—History of Maryland—
Government and politics—Economy and resources—People and culture—Timeline—
State flag and seal.
    ISBN 0–7368–1588–0 (hardcover)
    1. Maryland—Juvenile literature. [1. Maryland.] I. Title II. Series.
    F181.3 .P45 2003
    917.52—dc21   2002010268

Summary: An introduction to the geography, history, government, politics, economy,
resources, people, and culture of Maryland, including maps, charts, and a recipe.

Editorial Credits

Katy Kudela, editor; Jennifer Schonborn, series and book designer; Angi Gahler, illustrator;
    Karrey Tweten, photo researcher; Eric Kudalis, product planning editor

Photo Credits

Cover images: St. Mary's Church and State House, Annapolis, Michael Townsend;
historic barn in Bachman Mills, Carroll County, Stephen McDaniel

Allen Blake Sheldon, 56; Art Resource/Edward Owen, 28–29; Bruce Coleman, Inc./Michael
Ventura, 32; Capstone Press/Gary Sundermeyer, 54; Corbis, 38; Corbis/Bettmann, 25, 26;
Corbis/Lowell Georgia, 4; Corbis/Paul A. Souders, 10, 40, 53; Corbis/Richard T. Nowitz,
42–43; Digital Stock, 13; Hulton/Archive by Getty Images, 18, 52; Hulton/Archive by
Getty Images/CNP/Archive Photos, 35; Index Stock Imagery/Mark Gibson, 46; North
Wind Picture Archives, 21, 22, 58; One Mile Up, Inc., 55 (both); Panoramic Images/Jason
Horowitz, 50–51; Pat & Chuck Blackley, 17; PhotoDisc, Inc., 1, 48; Robert McCaw, 57;
Stephen McDaniel, 8, 63; Steve Mulligan, 14–15; UNICORN Stock Photos/Andre Jenny,
44; UNICORN Stock Photos/
Mary Morina, 31; U.S. Postal Service, 59

Artistic Elements

Brand X Pictures; Corbis; PhotoDisc, Inc.

1 2 3 4 5 6 08 07 06 05 04 03

Table of Contents

The skipjack is Maryland's state boat. Sailors use these boats to gather oysters from the bay.

Chapter 1

About Maryland

In the early morning hours, sailors board their boats on the Chesapeake Bay. They are ready for a day of gathering oysters. The work is difficult and tiring. These sailors often face cold temperatures and high winds.

Oysters are an important part of Maryland's seafood industry. The oyster season begins in October and ends in March. Many sailors scoop oysters from the bottom of the bay. Others dive for oysters just as American Indians once did.

A few sailors sail skipjacks across the bay. These small sailboats drag a net along the bottom of the bay to gather oysters. Sailors first used skipjacks during the late 1890s. These easy-to-build boats became a popular way to harvest oysters. Today, fewer than a dozen of these boats still operate.

Chesapeake Bay has always supplied jobs to Marylanders. The state's shipbuilding industry began in colonial times and continues today. The bay's seafood industry also employs many people. Since 1990, Chesapeake Bay has produced about 50 million pounds of seafood each year.

The Old Line State

People often call Maryland the "Old Line State." During the Revolutionary War (1775–1783), Maryland's troops fought in many battles. These soldiers were called the Maryland Line. General George Washington praised the soldiers for their bravery. Many historians believe Washington nicknamed the state the Old Line State.

Maryland is a small state. Pennsylvania borders Maryland to the north. Both Delaware and the Atlantic Ocean lie on

Maryland Cities

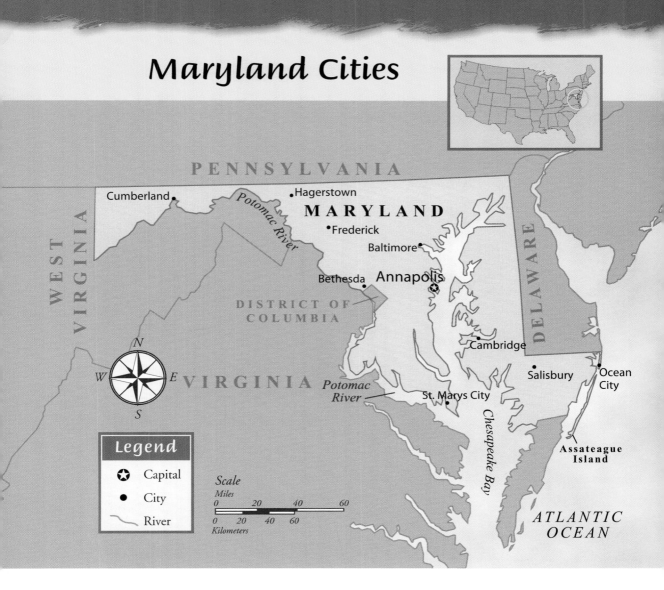

Maryland's eastern border. Virginia is to the south, and
West Virginia borders Maryland to the southwest and west.
Washington, D.C., is located between Maryland and
Virginia. The nation's capital was once a part of Maryland.

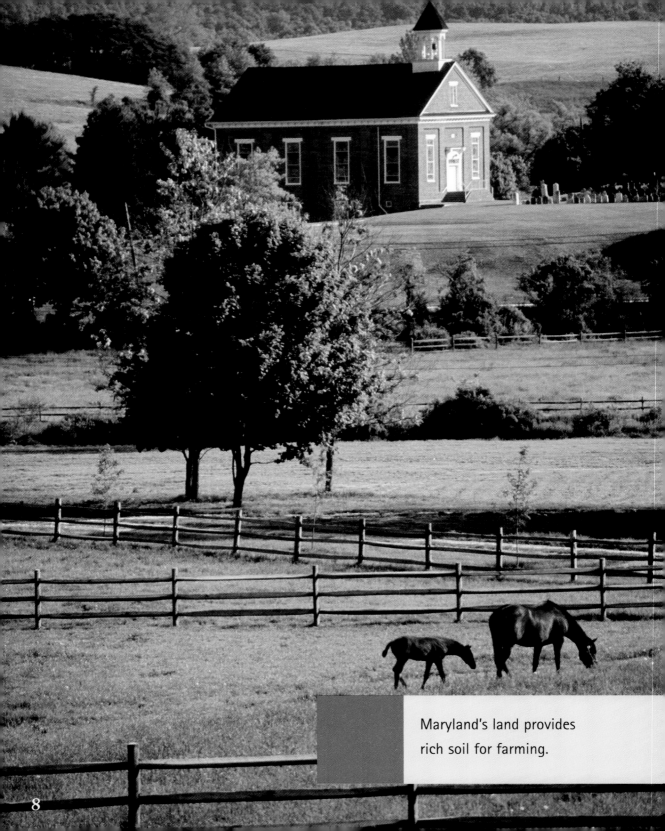

Maryland's land provides rich soil for farming.

Chapter 2

Land, Climate, and Wildlife

Maryland is one of the mid-Atlantic states. The state has five natural land regions. The Coastal Plain region is located in the east. The Piedmont region is in the center of the state. The Ridge and Valley, the Blue Ridge, and the Appalachian Plateau regions are found in the west.

Some people divide Maryland into six regions. The sixth region is the Atlantic Continental Shelf. Assateague Island is located in this area.

Coastal Plain Region

The Coastal Plain region surrounds the broad Chesapeake Bay and stretches west along the Potomac River. The Potomac River flows past Washington, D.C. The river forms the southern border of the state.

The Coastal Plain is flat and sometimes swampy on the east side of the bay. This area is part of the Delmarva Peninsula. The west side of the bay is covered with low, rolling hills. The cities of Baltimore, Ocean City, Salisbury, and Washington, D.C., are located in the coastal region.

Chesapeake Bay is one of Maryland's best known features. Melted glacier ice formed the bay more than 10,000 years ago.

Maryland's Land Features

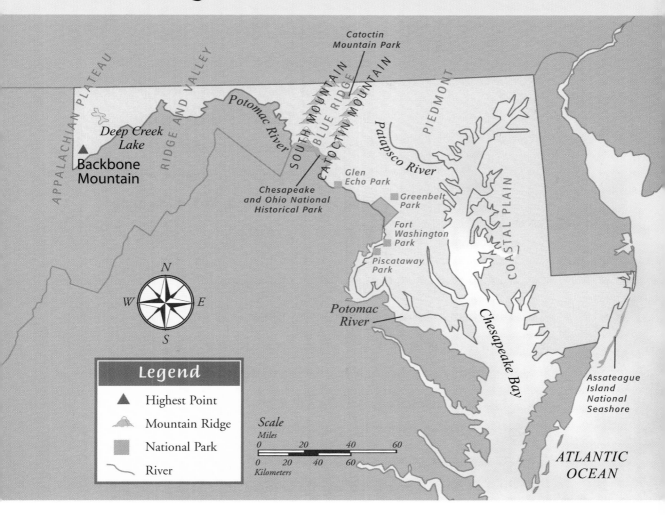

Catoctin
Mountain Park

APPALACHIAN PLATEAU

RIDGE AND VALLEY

Potomac River

SOUTH MOUNTAIN

BLUE RIDGE

CATOCTIN MOUNTAIN

PIEDMONT

Patapsco River

COASTAL PLAIN

Deep Creek
Lake

Backbone
Mountain

Chesapeake
and Ohio National
Historical Park

Glen
Echo Park

Greenbelt
Park

Fort
Washington
Park

Piscataway
Park

Potomac
River

Chesapeake Bay

Assateague
Island
National
Seashore

N
W   E
S

ATLANTIC
OCEAN

Legend

▲ Highest Point

🏔 Mountain Ridge

▪ National Park

〜 River

Scale
Miles
0   20   40   60

0   20   40   60
Kilometers

Much of Maryland's coastline lies along Chesapeake Bay. The state also has 30 miles (48 kilometers) of coast along the Atlantic Ocean. Assateague Island is located offshore. This island belongs to both Maryland and Virginia.

Chesapeake Bay is the largest ocean bay in the United States. The bay's main basin reaches about 200 miles (322 kilometers) from Havre de Grace, Maryland, to Norfolk, Virginia. The bay is very shallow. Its deepest point is less than 175 feet (53 meters).

Piedmont and Blue Ridge Regions

The Piedmont region is a series of rolling hills and valleys. Two main ridges in this area are Parrs Ridge and Dug Hill Ridge. These ridges stretch northeast to southwest. Many dairy farms are in this area. The Patapsco River flows from the Piedmont Region into Chesapeake Bay.

The Blue Ridge region has two mountain ridges, which are split by the Middletown Valley. Catoctin Mountain is on the east side of the valley. On the west side is South Mountain, which stretches into Virginia.

Ridge and Valley Region

The Ridge and Valley region includes the wide Hagerstown Valley as well as forested ridges and deep, narrow valleys. Hagerstown Valley is about 20 miles (32 kilometers) wide. The ridges of this farming area run northeast to southwest and rise as high as 2,000 feet (610 meters).

Appalachian Plateau Region

The Appalachian Plateau rises in the far western area of the state. Forested mountains and steep-sided river valleys are

About 41 percent of Maryland's land is covered with forests.

found in this area. Backbone Mountain, the state's highest point, stands 3,360 feet (1,024 meters) above sea level.

Maryland has no natural lakes, but dams have created lakes and reservoirs. Maryland's largest lake, Deep Creek Lake, is in this area. The lake measures 7 square miles (18 square kilometers).

Climate

Maryland has mostly hot, humid summers and cool winters. An average summer temperature in Maryland is 73 degrees

Fahrenheit (22.7 degrees Celsius.) During the winter, Maryland's average temperature is 34 degrees Fahrenheit (1.1 degrees Celsius.)

Maryland receives an average of 43 inches (109 centimeters) of rain and snow. The state receives more than half of its precipitation in the summer.

Forests and Wildlife

Maryland's forests include white oak, maple, and hickory trees. The Wye Oak was Maryland's most famous tree.

The Appalachian Plateau region is in western Maryland. Forested mountains cover much of this area's land.

"I was deeply saddened tonight to learn of the loss of one of our state's most historic, beautiful and stately natural resources. For more than 450 years, the Wye Oak has stood strong and tall, surviving winds, drought and diseases of nature, and even more remarkably, the human threats of chain saws and global warming."

—Parris N. Glendening, governor of Maryland

The Wye Oak stood in Wye Mills, Maryland, for more than 450 years. The tree measured 106 feet (32 meters). It was the largest white oak in the United States. A thunderstorm on June 6, 2002, took down the famous tree.

Maryland's forests, wetlands, and waters are home to a number of small mammals, birds, and reptiles. White-tailed deer, red foxes, and gray squirrels are a few of the animals found in the state.

Loss of habitat has greatly reduced the numbers of some of Maryland's animals. As settlers cleared Maryland's forests for farmland, many black bears lost their homes. In 1956, reports showed only 12 black bears in the state. The state took action to protect the bears. Today, more than 300 black bears live in the state. Other animals also are threatened. Turtles called diamondback terrapins make their home on Maryland's beaches. A loss of nesting areas has led to fewer terrapins in the state. The state is trying to save these turtles.

Assateague Island

Wild ponies have roamed Assateague Island for more than 200 years. No one is quite sure how the wild ponies came to the island. Several legends have tried to explain this event.

According to one legend, a Spanish ship sank off Maryland's coast sometime during the 1600s. A herd of horses was aboard the ship. When the ship started to sink, the horses swam ashore to the island. Another story claims that the ponies descended from horses brought to shore by Spanish pirates.

Historians believe that farmers placed many of the horses on the island. The island provided farmers with free pastures. The farmers also avoided livestock taxes and the expense of building fences.

Two herds of wild ponies now live on the 37-mile-long (60-kilometer-long) island. Visitors to the island may see the ponies roaming the beaches, roadways, campgrounds, and marsh areas.

George Calvert received land in Maryland from King Charles I. He hoped to start a new home for his family.

Chapter 3

History of Maryland

Around A.D. 1200, American Indians began to build villages in Maryland. The Potomac, Susquehannock, and Nanticoke were three of the tribal groups living in Maryland.

In 1608, Captain John Smith of the Jamestown colony in Virginia explored the Chesapeake Bay area. Settlers in Virginia soon traveled to Maryland to trade with the American Indians. In 1631, William Claiborne built a trading post on Kent Island in the Chesapeake Bay.

Start of a Colony

In 1632, England's King Charles I promised George Calvert a grant of land. Calvert held the title Lord Baltimore. The land was located north of Maryland's Potomac River. King Charles asked Calvert to name the new colony after his wife, Queen Henrietta Maria. The Calverts named the colony Maryland.

At the time, Roman Catholics were being punished in England. The Calverts were Catholic. They wanted to find a place where they could worship in peace.

George Calvert died a few months before receiving the land grant. His son, Cecilius, became the second Lord Baltimore. Cecilius sent his brother, Leonard, to Maryland.

Leonard Calvert led a group of more than 130 people to Maryland. The group's two ships, the *Ark* and the *Dove*, landed on Maryland's coast on March 25, 1634. As the first governor of Maryland, Leonard founded St. Marys City as the capital.

Colony Faces Many Changes

The settlers in Calvert's group soon began farming. William Claiborne was not happy about the settlers moving into the area. Claiborne and others began to create problems for the colony.

During the next 50 years, the Maryland colony suffered from political and religious troubles. The colony

St. Marys City became the colonists new home. They cleared the forests for farming and traded with the American Indians.

changed leaders several times. In 1692, King William of England took control of the colony. He moved the capital to Anne Arundel. The name of the city was changed to Annapolis in honor of Princess Anne, daughter of Queen Mary. The Calverts took back control of the colony in 1715.

As the colony grew, tobacco became the main crop. Landowners needed many workers to work in the tobacco fields. African American slaves became the main source of farm labor. In response to the demand for labor, Maryland's legislature passed laws allowing slavery.

By the early 1700s, Baltimore's natural harbor became a shipping center. Its fast-flowing streams drove water wheels that powered flour mills.

The Maryland colonists saw a new group of settlers arrive during the 1730s. Many German immigrants moved into

During the 1700s, Baltimore grew as a shipping center. The seafood and shipping industry helped the city grow quickly.

western Maryland. Most of the state's American Indians were forced to leave.

Troubles in the Colony

During this time, colonists in Maryland and Pennsylvania argued over state borders. Between 1763 and 1767, two Englishmen named Charles Mason and Jeremiah Dixon studied the area. They drew a boundary later known as the Mason-Dixon Line.

In 1765, Great Britain tightened its control over the colonies by passing the Stamp Act. This law angered many colonists because it made them pay taxes on goods and services. In May 1773, England passed the Tea Act. This law forced colonists to pay taxes on tea from England.

In response to the Tea Act, a group of citizens in Boston, Massachusetts, dumped tea from a British ship into the Boston Harbor. This event is known as the Boston Tea Party. England then passed the Boston Port Act. This law punished all the people of Boston by closing the port and letting Great Britain take firmer control.

In October 1774, a ship named *Peggy Stewart* arrived in Annapolis. The ship carried 2,000 pounds (1.8 metric tons) of tea on which the tax had been paid. A group from Maryland burned the ship in protest of the Boston Port Act.

Revolutionary War

Maryland joined the American Revolution in June 1776. The following month, the Declaration of Independence was signed in Philadelphia. The 13 colonies declared themselves free of British rule.

During the Revolutionary War, many Maryland ship owners changed their ships to warships. The ships, called privateers, were used in battle against the British Navy.

In 1776, Marylanders wrote their first state constitution. The following year, Thomas Johnson was elected the first governor under the state constitution.

Following the war, the 13 colonies formed a new government. They created the Articles of Confederation. Maryland became the seventh state of the union on April 28, 1788.

War of 1812

Troubles between the United States and Britain resulted in the War of 1812 (1812–1814). In August 1814, British

Fort McHenry was heavily attacked by
the British navy during the War of 1812.

troops marched up the Potomac River and burned
Washington, D.C. The British then marched down the
river to try to capture Baltimore.

On September 12, 1814, Marylanders fought the British
army at North Point, just below Baltimore. The British navy

attacked Fort McHenry. U.S. soldiers guarded Baltimore's harbor nonstop for one day and one night.

On the morning of September 14, Francis Scott Key saw that the U.S. flag was still flying over Fort McHenry. That afternoon, the British navy gave up and sailed away. Key wrote a poem about the battle. Key's "The Star Spangled Banner" became the U.S. national anthem in 1931.

Francis Scott Key wrote a poem about the battle at Fort McHenry. This poem became the United State's national anthem, "The Star Spangled Banner."

"There was one of two things I had a right to, liberty or death. If I could not have one, I would have the other."
—*Harriet Tubman, born into slavery in Maryland, she escaped slavery and later led slaves to freedom on the Underground Railroad*

Slavery in the United States

During the late 1800s, slavery once again became a national issue for the United States. The Mason-Dixon Line marked the line between the North and South. Many people in the North believed slavery was wrong, while many people in the South disagreed.

Maryland was south of the Mason-Dixon Line, but was divided on the issue of slavery. Some people favored slavery because their businesses profited from it. Others favored the Union ideas of human rights.

The North and South continued to argue over slavery. In 1860 and 1861, 11 Southern states seceded from the United States. They formed the Confederate States of America.

Civil War

The Civil War (1861-1865) began on April 12, 1861. President Abraham Lincoln used military force to keep Maryland from becoming a Confederate state. He stationed Union troops in the state.

Maryland remained in the Union. But a large number
of Marylanders fought for the Confederacy.

The Civil War brought two major battles to Maryland.
On September 14, 1862, Union soldiers defeated Confederate
troops at South Mountain. On September 17, the two armies
met again at the Battle of Antietam.

The Battle of Antietam is known as the bloodiest day
in American history. Historians estimate that more than
23,000 soldiers were killed, went missing, or were wounded
during this battle.

Railroad Strikes

After the Civil War, troubles continued in Maryland. In 1877, the Baltimore & Ohio (B&O) Railroad cut the pay of its workers. Railroad workers went on strike, refusing to work. A Pennsylvania army was sent in to stop the strike. A group of Baltimore citizens attacked the army. The strike spread to other railroads.

About 100,000 U.S. railroad workers went on strike. During the national strike, 100 people were killed and 1,000 workers were jailed.

The Battle of Antietam is often called the bloodiest day in U.S. history. During the battle, Union soldiers stopped the Confederate army from going north of Washington, D.C.

Fight for Equal Rights

A fight for civil rights had begun in Maryland's early years. Marylanders continued their fight for civil rights. During World War II (1939–1945), factory and business owners needed workers. Many African Americans found jobs. When the war ended, many African American workers and women were asked to give up their jobs. Factory owners wanted to give jobs back to the white men returning from the war.

African Americans protested. The Baltimore branch of the National Association for the Advancement of Colored People (NAACP) fought for equal rights.

During the 1960s, Marylanders' efforts to end segregation caused problems. Many people wanted to keep whites and African Americans separated. They did not believe African Americans should receive the same rights as whites. Race riots broke out in Cambridge in 1963 and 1964. Segregation laws began to change. In Maryland, these changes opened public schools, pools, and parks to African Americans.

Over the years, Maryland passed laws to give equal rights to its citizens. By the late 1970s, Maryland had one of the highest percentages of African American and female legislators.

Harborplace brings many visitors to Baltimore. The city's cleanup efforts have turned Baltimore into a model for other cities.

Citizens Work Together

In the 1970s, Marylanders made efforts to improve Baltimore. New homeowners could buy old and abandoned houses for a dollar. Buyers repaired the houses. The neighborhoods grew. In 1980, city leaders created Harborplace in the Inner Harbor. This area has stores, restaurants, and office buildings.

Maryland's capitol building is the only state capitol to have served as the nation's capitol.

Government and Politics

Marylanders have long debated over religion and civil rights. One important religious debate took place in the early 1800s. In 1817, Scottish settler Thomas Kennedy became a member of the Maryland House of Delegates.

At the time, about 150 Jewish people lived in the state. Legally, Jews were not full citizens. The mistreatment of Jews angered Kennedy. He believed religion was a private matter. He also believed all people should have equal rights.

Kennedy introduced a bill to give Jews equal rights. His actions angered many people. He lost an election for the House of Delegates, but won the next election two years later.

In 1826, Kennedy's bill finally passed. Within a few months, two Jewish citizens were elected to the Baltimore City Council.

Kennedy served the people of Hagerstown until he died in 1832. A monument in Hagerstown reads, "One who loved his fellow man."

Important Laws

Throughout its history, Maryland's government has led the nation in creating important laws. In 1649, Lord Baltimore pushed the Maryland legislature to pass the Act Concerning Religion. This act was one of the first laws that promised freedom of religion.

In 1906, Maryland passed a law to help disabled workers. The law made an insurance fund for disabled workers. It also said employers are responsible for the safety of their workers. After many court challenges by businesses, a final law was passed in 1916.

Fight for Equality

Baltimore attorney Thurgood Marshall led the national fight against segregated schools. In 1954, Marshall won the case *Brown v. Board of Education of Topeka* before the U.S. Supreme Court. The Supreme Court ruled that segregated schools were unequal. Public schools opened to students of all races.

Marshall later became the first African American Supreme Court justice. He served in this role from 1967 to 1991.

State Constitution

Maryland adopted its current constitution in 1867. The state adopted earlier constitutions in 1776, 1851, and 1864.

In 1967, the legislature held a special convention to create a new constitution. Despite the lawmakers work, voters decided to keep the constitution from 1867.

State Government

Maryland's government has three branches. They are the executive branch, the legislative branch, and the judicial branch.

The governor heads the executive branch. Other elected officials in the executive branch include the lieutenant governor, the attorney general, the secretary of state, and the comptroller of the treasury.

The state legislature is called the General Assembly. It has two parts, the Senate and the House of Delegates. One senator is elected from each of Maryland's 47 legislative districts. The House of Delegates has 141 members.

The judicial branch is headed by the Court of Appeals. The second highest court in Maryland is the court of special appeals. The state's circuit courts handle both civil and criminal cases. The district court handles minor civil and criminal matters and motor vehicle law.

During national elections, Maryland usually votes Democratic. Maryland has eight representatives and two senators in Washington, D.C. Maryland casts 10 electoral votes in presidential elections.

Maryland's State Government

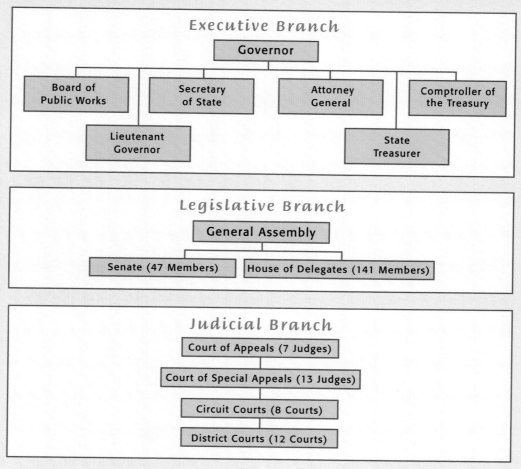

There are 23 counties in Maryland. Boards of county commissioners govern more than half of the counties. County councils govern the remaining counties.

Dairy cattle are an important part of Maryland's economy.

Chapter 5

Economy and Resources

When settlers first arrived in Maryland, they cleared the forests for farms. Farming was the state's main business until the 1800s. Later, Maryland became known as a shipping center. Today, the major industries are agriculture, transportation, and manufacturing.

Agriculture

Agriculture has always been an important part of Maryland. Tobacco was the most important crop until the mid-1900s. In recent years, increased knowledge about the dangers of smoking have caused problems for the industry.

Famous Blue Crabs

Blue crabs are a delicious and valuable shellfish that live in the Chesapeake Bay. The Chesapeake Bay's mixture of fresh and salt water is a perfect home for these creatures.

Some Marylanders catch crabs for a living. They use baited traps called "crab pots." Other people catch crabs as a hobby. They use a hand net and a baited line. In recent years, some people have feared that crabs are overfished. The state plans to protect the crabs for future generations.

Today, milk, eggs, and other livestock products are the state's major farm products. Farmers raise beef cattle and hogs in western Maryland.

Crops are another important part of Maryland's agriculture. Most corn is grown in the Piedmont region, while soybeans are raised on the eastern shore. Apples, peaches, pears, plums, and cherries are grown in western Maryland. The climate on the eastern shore is ideal for growing peaches, strawberries, and watermelons. Shrubs, flowers, and other plants are also important crops.

Fishing and Logging

Fishing continues to add to the state's economy. The waters of the Chesapeake Bay provide crabs, oysters, and fish.

Forests cover about 41 percent of Maryland. Forests provide wood to make homes, furniture, and paper products.

Manufacturing

Maryland was one of the nation's first manufacturing centers. The natural harbor on the Chesapeake Bay allowed ships to easily transport Maryland's products to other states and countries.

Maryland continues to be a national manufacturing center. Today, products manufactured in the state include chemicals, metals, industrial machinery, and navigation equipment.

Transportation

Maryland was one of the nation's first transportation centers. The first regular stagecoach line began running between Baltimore and Philadelphia in 1773. In 1828, construction on

the B&O Railroad began in Maryland. The B&O was the nation's first railroad.

Transportation is still important to Maryland. Sparrows Point, Maryland, is one of the main U.S. shipbuilding and repair centers. Fishing boats and other small craft are built and repaired at boatyards throughout the Chesapeake Bay area. Baltimore is still one of the major ports of the United States.

The natural harbor in Baltimore has helped the city's growth. The harbor is used for both recreation and industry. More than 6 million tons of cargo pass through the harbor each year.

Annapolis is home to the U.S. Naval Academy.

Service Industries

About 80 percent of Maryland's people work in service industries. Service workers have jobs in tourism, retail, government, real estate, and other businesses. Most of these jobs are located in and around Washington, D.C., and Baltimore. The U.S. federal government is one of the state's largest employers.

Universities and Research

Maryland has a history of supporting schools and education. In 1696, King William's School opened in Maryland. This school was one of America's first public schools. Today, it is a university called St. John's College. The U.S. Naval Academy is located in Annapolis.

Maryland universities have been leaders in education and research. In 1876, Johns Hopkins University opened its doors in Baltimore. Since then, it has been a leader in medical research and education. The university system in Maryland has 13 institutions, with an enrollment of more than 130,000 students.

Annapolis is Maryland's capital city. The downtown area of this city offers visitors and residents shops and restaurants.

Chapter 6

People and Culture

Waves of immigrants came to Maryland from Europe during the 1700s and 1800s. Today, members of many ethnic groups live in Maryland, including African Americans, Asians, Hispanics or Latinos, and American Indians.

The state capital, Annapolis, has about 36,000 people. More than half of Marylanders live in medium-sized cities and towns, such as Columbia, Frederick, Hagerstown, and Silver Spring. Many live in cities near Baltimore. Many more live in cities surrounding Washington, D.C. About a third of Maryland's people live in small towns or in rural areas.

Charm City

Maryland has only one large city. Baltimore is home to about 651,000 people.

People often call Baltimore the "Charm City" because it has many interesting neighborhoods and historic places.

Tourists can find many places to visit in Baltimore, including Fort McHenry, the Babe Ruth Museum, and the Maryland Science Center. Visitors to Baltimore's Inner Harbor can see the Baltimore National Aquarium, Harborplace, and many other attractions. In the future, the state plans to open the Reginald F. Lewis Maryland Museum of African American History and Culture, in the Inner Harbor area.

Maryland's Ethnic Backgrounds

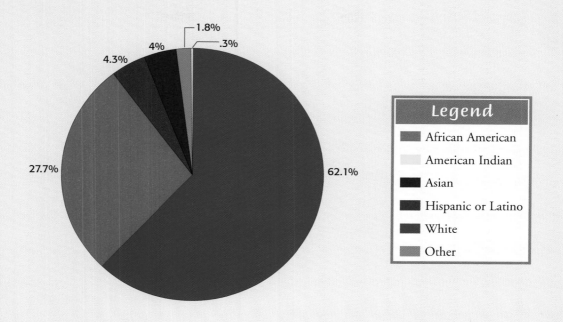

1.8%
.3%
4%
4.3%
27.7%
62.1%

Legend
- African American
- American Indian
- Asian
- Hispanic or Latino
- White
- Other

Proud of State History

On March 25, schools in Maryland celebrate Maryland Day. This holiday honors the day settlers from the *Ark* and the *Dove* landed on Maryland soil.

Maryland Day began in 1903. Schools throughout the state set aside the day to remember the state's history. The holiday grew in popularity. In 1916, the legislature named Maryland Day a legal holiday.

"As I grew up here, I not only had dreams of being a big league ballplayer, but also of being a Baltimore Oriole.
—Cal Ripken Jr., former Baltimore Oriole, born in Maryland

Sports and Pastimes

Marylanders play several sports not often seen in the rest of the United States. Jousting is the state's official sport. Jousters charge on horseback with a lance and try to put the lance's tip through a ring hanging from a ribbon.

Duckpin bowling was invented in 1900 by Baltimore Oriole baseball stars John J. McGraw and Wilbert Robinson. The game they invented is still popular throughout the state. This sport is played with a small ball and short pins. Bowlers are given three balls per turn. The game is scored like regular bowling.

Other sports are also important to Marylanders. The state is home to a major league baseball team, the Baltimore Orioles, and four minor league baseball teams. Babe Ruth,

Baseball is a favorite pastime for many residents in Maryland. The state's major league baseball team is the Baltimore Orioles.

What is in a Name?

In 1996, Maryland sports fans saw the return of pro football. Baltimore fans named their new team the Ravens in honor of American poet, Edgar Allan Poe. While living in Baltimore, Poe wrote the poem *The Raven*.

Poe became famous for his poems and horror stories. *The Purloined Letter* was the first detective story. Among Poe's most famous poems are *The Raven* and *The Bells*.

Cal Ripken Jr., and many other famous baseball players were born in the state.

Football has been popular in Maryland since the 1890s. The Baltimore Colts were the state's popular professional NFL team from 1953 to 1983.

In 1984, a new owner took the Colts to Indianapolis. For 13 years, fans gathered in parking lots and auditoriums on Sundays to relive old memories and hear the Colts marching band play. In 1996, Baltimore got a new NFL team when the Ravens came to town. The Ravens won the Super Bowl in 2001.

America in Miniature

"America in Miniature" is a phrase used to describe the state of Maryland. Although small in size, the state has every type of natural feature except a desert. Many key events in U.S. history have occurred in Maryland.

Maryland is a state with unique cultural and recreational activities. The state's culture and climate will continue to be the special features of the Old Line State.

Jousting is the state sport in Maryland. It is just one of the many unique activities found in the state.

Recipe: Strawberry Ice Cream

Maryland has many dairy farms. In 1998, milk became the state drink. Ice cream has been a popular dairy treat in Maryland for many years. In 1851, Jacob Fussell started the first commercial ice cream business in Baltimore.

Ingredients

16 ounces (455 grams) half and half
½ cup (120 mL) sugar
1 teaspoon (5 mL) vanilla
½ cup (120 mL) frozen, unsweetened, sliced strawberries
1 5-pound (2.25-kilogram) bag of small ice cubes
2 cups (480 mL) salt

Equipment

liquid measuring cups
measuring spoons
1 small coffee can
1 large coffee can
wooden spoon
pot holders

What You Do

1. Put half and half, sugar, vanilla, and strawberries in the small, clean coffee can.

2. Stir the above ingredients together with a wooden spoon.

3. Place the lid tightly on the small can.

4. Put the small coffee can in the middle of the large, clean coffee can.

5. Place ice around the small can. The ice should fill the large can.

6. Pour 1 cup (250 mL) of salt over the ice.

7. Seal the lid tightly on the large can.

8. Using pot holders, roll the can around on the floor for 10 minutes.

9. After 10 minutes, take the small can out of the large can. Have an adult help you to remove the lid and stir the ice cream mixture with a wooden spoon.

10. Take the large can and pour out the ice and water into a sink.

11. Repeat steps 4, 5, 6, 7, 8, and 9.

12. Serve ice cream immediately or store ice cream in freezer.

Makes 4 to 6 servings

Maryland's Flag and Seal

Maryland's Flag

Maryland officially adopted its state flag in 1904. Maryland's flag contains the black and gold crest of the Calvert family and the red and white crest of the Crossland family. The Crosslands were the family of George Calvert's mother.

Maryland's State Seal

The seal of Maryland has two sides. The side used officially has a shield with the Calvert and Crossland coats of arms. Above the coats of arms are an earl's coronet, or crown, and a full-faced knight's helmet. To the right and left of the shield stand a farmer and a fisherman. These figures symbolize Lord Baltimore's two estates which were Maryland and Avalon in Newfoundland, Canada.

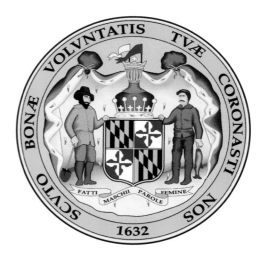

The seal's other side shows Lord Baltimore as a knight on a charging horse, waving a sword.

Almanac

General Facts

Nickname: The Old Line State

Population: 5,296,486 (U.S. Census Bureau, 2000)

Population rank: 19th

Capital: Annapolis

Largest cities: Baltimore, Frederick, Gaithersburg, Bowie, Rockville

Geography

Area: 12,407 square miles (32,134 square kilometers)

Size rank: 42nd

Highest point: Backbone Mountain, 3,360 feet (1,024 meters) above sea level

Lowest point: Atlantic Ocean, sea level

Agriculture

Agricultural products: Chickens, corn, dairy products, soybeans, greenhouse products

Climate

Average winter temperature: 34 degrees Fahrenheit (1.1 degrees Celsius)

Average summer temperature: 73 degrees Fahrenheit (23 degrees Celsius)

Average annual precipitation: 43 inches (109 centimeters)

Diamondback terrapin

Baltimore oriole

Bird: Baltimore oriole

Cat: Calico cat

Dog: Chesapeake Bay retriever

Flower: Black-eyed Susan

Economy

Natural resources:
Sand and gravel, forests

Types of industry:
Foodstuffs, computers
and electronics,
transportation
equipment, steel,
metal products

Symbols

Reptile: Diamondback
terrapin

Song: "Maryland, My
Maryland," by James
Ryder Randall

Sport: Jousting

Tree: White oak

Government

First governor: Thomas
Johnson

Statehood: April 28, 1788
(7th state)

U.S. Representatives: 8

U.S. Senators: 2

U.S. electoral votes: 10

Counties: 23

Timeline

State History

Early 1600s
Settlers in Virginia travel to Maryland to trade with American Indians.

1632
King Charles I grants Maryland land charter to George Calvert.

1634
Ark and *Dove* arrive in Maryland; settlers found St. Marys City.

1788
Maryland becomes the seventh state.

1867
The present Maryland state constitution is adopted.

1862
Union and Confederate troops fight the Battle of Antietam on September 17.

U.S. History

1620
Pilgrims settle in Plymouth, Massachusetts.

1775–1783
The Revolutionary War begins in 1775.

1812–1814
The United States and Great Britain fight the War of 1812.

1861–1865
The Civil War between the North and South begins in 1861.

1954
Thurgood Marshall wins U.S. Supreme Court case ending segregated schools.

2002
A thunderstorm takes down Maryland's 450-year-old Wye Oak tree.

1980
The city of Baltimore opens Harborplace.

1929–1939
The United States experiences the Great Depression.

Sept. 11, 2001
Terrorists attack the World Trade Center and Pentagon.

1939–1945
World War II is fought; the United States enters the war in 1941.

1964
The U.S. Congress approves the Civil Rights Act, making discrimination illegal.

1914–1918
World War I is fought; the United States enters the war in 1917.

Words to Know

civil rights (SIV-il RITES)—the rights that all people have to freedom and equal treatment under the law

jousting (JOUST-ing)—a sport performed on horseback with a lance

precipitation (pri-sip-i-TAY-shuhn)—the rain and snow an area receives

privateer (PRYE-vuh-teer)—a private ship that is authorized to attack enemy ships during wartime

reservoir (REZ-ur-vwar)—a natural or artificial structure that is a holding area for a large amount of water

secession (si-SESH-uhn)—the act of withdrawing from or leaving an organization; in U.S. history, secession was the withdrawal of 11 Southern states from the Union.

segregation (seg-ruh-GAY-shuhn)—the policy of separating people according to their race

skipjack (SKIP-jak)—a small, single-masted sailboat; the skipjack is the state boat of Maryland.

strike (STRIKE)—to refuse to work until a set of demands is met

terrapin (TER-uh-pin)—a North American turtle; the diamondback terrapin is Maryland's state reptile.

To Learn More

Burgan, Michael. *Maryland*. America the Beautiful. New York: Children's Press, 1999.

Gregson, Susan R. *Francis Scott Key: Patriotic Poet*. Let Freedom Ring. Mankato, Minn.: Bridgestone Books, 2003.

Maynard, Charles W. *Fort McHenry*. Famous Forts Throughout American History. New York: Rosen Publishing, 2002.

Pietrzyk, Leslie. *Maryland*. Celebrate the States. New York: Benchmark Books, 2000.

Internet Sites

Track down many sites about Maryland.
Visit the FACT HOUND at *http://www.facthound.com*

IT IS EASY! IT IS FUN!
1) Go to *http://www.facthound.com*
2) Type in: 0736815880
3) Click on "FETCH IT" and FACT
   HOUND will find several
   links hand-picked by our editors.

Relax and let our pal FACT HOUND do the research for you!

Places to Write and Visit

Chesapeake Bay Maritime Museum
Mill Street
P.O. Box 636
St. Michaels, MD 21663

Maryland Historical Society
201 West Monument Street
Baltimore, MD 21201–4674

Maryland Office of Tourism
217 East Redwood Street, 9th Floor
Baltimore, MD 21202

U.S. Naval Academy
121 Blake Road
Annapolis, MD 21402–5000

Maryland's Wye Oak tree stood for more than 450 years in Wye Oak Mills.

Index